CW00421618

Saturday Night Meals

Delicious Meals for the Weekends

By
BookSumo Press

Published by
http://www.booksumo.com

Table of Contents

Texas Style Fried Chicken 25

Sweet Honey Chicken 27

Texas Mexican Burritos 28

Carolina Sweet Chicken 29

Authentic Southern Corn 30

Buttermilk Paprika Fried Chicken 31

Southern Louisiana Vegetable Medley 32

Tex Mex Shrimp 33

Southern Macaroni and Cheese 34

New England Style Clam Chowder 35

New England Fried Chips and Fried Fish 36

Fettuccini Shrimp & Scallions 37

Yankee Fried Honey and Garlic Chicken 38

Manhattan Style Cheesecake 39

Classical Baked Beans from Boston 40

Authentic Eggplant Parmesan 41

Authentic Meatball Sub 42

Italian Pepper and Pasta 43

Dijon Downstate Chicken 44

Manhattan Island Burgers 45

Pepperjack Pizza

Prep Time: 20 mins
Total Time: 32 mins

Servings per Recipe: 6	
Calories	373 kcal
Fat	15.3 g
Carbohydrates	44g
Protein	17 g
Cholesterol	26 mg
Sodium	1027 mg

Ingredients

1/2 (16 oz.) can spicy fat-free refried beans
1 C. salsa, divided
1 (12 inch) pre-baked Italian pizza crust
2 C. shredded hearts of romaine lettuce
3 medium green onions, thinly sliced

1/4 C. ranch dressing
1/4 C. crumbled tortilla chips
1 C. shredded pepper Jack cheese

Directions

1. Set your oven to 450 degrees F before doing anything else and arrange a rack in the lowest portion of the oven.
2. In a bowl, mix together the beans and 1/2 C. of the salsa.
3. Arrange the crust on a cookie sheet and top with the bean mixture evenly.
4. Cook in the oven for about 10 minutes.
5. Remove from the oven and place the lettuce, green onions over the beans mixture.
6. Top with the remaining salsa.
7. Drizzle with the dressing evenly and top with the chips and cheese venly.
8. Cook in the oven for about 2 minutes more.
9. Cut into 6 slices and serve.

WEEKEND
Taco Lasagna

🥘 Prep Time: 25 mins

🕐 Total Time: 45 mins

Servings per Recipe: 5

Calories	447 kcal
Fat	24 g
Carbohydrates	33.2g
Protein	23.2 g
Cholesterol	79 mg
Sodium	899 mg

Ingredients

1 lb. lean ground beef
1 (1 oz.) package taco seasoning mix
1 (14 oz.) can peeled and diced tomatoes with juice
10 (6 inch) corn tortillas

1 C. prepared salsa
1/2 C. shredded Colby cheese

Directions

1. Set your oven to 350 degrees F before doing anything else.
2. Heat a large skillet on medium-high heat and cook the beef till browned completely.
3. Stir in the taco seasoning and tomatoes.
4. In the bottom of a 13x9-inch baking dish, arrange half of the tortillas evenly.
5. Place the beef mixture over the tortillas evenly.
6. Place the remaining tortillas over the beef mixture and top with the salsa, followed by the cheese.
7. Cook in the oven for about 20-30 minutes.

A Baked
Mexican Medley

Prep Time: 5 mins
Total Time: 1 hr 5 mins

Servings per Recipe: 8
Calories	480 kcal
Fat	26.6 g
Carbohydrates	24g
Protein	34.8 g
Cholesterol	104 mg
Sodium	1103 mg

Ingredients

1 (10.75 oz.) can condensed cream of mushroom soup
1 (10.75 oz.) can condensed cream of chicken soup
1 (4 oz.) can chopped green chili peppers, drained
1/4 C. milk
2/3 C. sour cream

8 (6 inch) flour tortillas
6 boneless chicken breast halves, cooked and cubed
2 C. shredded Cheddar cheese

Directions

1. Set your oven to 350 degrees F before doing anything else and lightly, grease a 13x9-inch baking dish.
2. In a medium bowl, add the cream of mushroom soup, cream of chicken soup, chili peppers, milk and sour cream and mix till well combined.
3. In the bottom of the prepared baking dish, arrange a layer of the tortilla strips.
4. Place 1/2 of the soup mixture, followed by 1/2 of the chicken and 1/2 of the shredded cheese.
5. Repeat the layers till all the ingredients are used completely, ending with a layer of the shredded cheese.
6. Cook, covered in the oven for about 45 minutes.
7. Uncover and cook for about 15 minutes more.

ELBOW
Macaroni Dinner

🥄 Prep Time: 10 mins
🕐 Total Time: 30 mins

Servings per Recipe: 6

Calories	588 kcal
Fat	20.4 g
Carbohydrates	70.6g
Protein	32.3 g
Cholesterol	76 mg
Sodium	1258 mg

Ingredients

1 lb. ground beef
1/2 onion, chopped
1 (12 oz.) package elbow macaroni
1/2 lb. processed cheese (such as Velveeta(R)), diced

1 1/2 C. salsa
1 (15 oz.) can pinto beans, drained and rinsed
1 (14 oz.) can whole kernel corn, drained

Directions

1. Heat a large skillet on medium heat and cook the beef and onion for about 10 minutes.
2. Drain the excess grease from the skillet.
3. Meanwhile in large pan of the lightly salted boiling water, cook the macaroni for about 8 minutes.
4. Drain well.
5. Add the macaroni in the pan with the beef mixture on medium-low heat.
6. Stir in the processed cheese for about 3 minutes.
7. Stir in the salsa, pinto beans and corn and cook for about 5 minutes.

Azteca
Tacos

🥣 Prep Time: 15 mins

🕐 Total Time: 25 mins

Servings per Recipe: 9

Calories	379 kcal
Fat	21.4 g
Carbohydrates	28.1g
Protein	20.3 g
Cholesterol	58 mg
Sodium	69 mg

Ingredients

2 lb. top sirloin steak, cut into thin strips
salt and ground black pepper to taste
1/4 C. vegetable oil
18 (6 inch) corn tortillas
1 onion, diced

4 fresh jalapeno peppers, seeded and chopped
1 bunch fresh cilantro, chopped
4 limes, cut into wedges

Directions

1. Heat a large skillet on medium-high heat and cook the steak for about 5 minutes.
2. Season with the salt and pepper and transfer into a plate and keep warm.
3. In the same skillet, heat the oil.
4. Place 1 tortilla in the hot oil and cook till browned lightly, turning once.
5. Repeat with the remaining tortillas.
6. Place the tortillas on a plate and top each one with the steak, onion, jalapeño and cilantro.
7. Drizzle with the lime juice.

CHIMICHANGAS

Prep Time: 20 mins
Total Time: 45 mins

Servings per Recipe: 6
Calories	1595 kcal
Fat	83.7 g
Carbohydrates	1133.4g
Protein	79.8 g
Cholesterol	1215 mg
Sodium	2322 mg

Ingredients

1 1/2 C. chicken broth
1 C. uncooked long-grain rice
1/2 C. red enchilada sauce
1 1/2 onion, diced, divided
6 (12 inch) flour tortillas
4 C. diced cooked chicken breast, divided
1 lb. Monterey Jack cheese, shredded, divided
1 (6 oz.) can sliced black olives
4 C. refried beans, divided
1/4 C. vegetable oil
TOPPING
3 avocados, peeled and pitted
1/2 C. finely chopped cilantro
2 tbsp lemon juice
3 green onions, diced
1/4 C. finely chopped jalapeno chili peppers
1 tomato, diced
2 C. shredded lettuce
1 C. sour cream
2 C. shredded Cheddar cheese

Directions

1. In a medium pan, mix together the broth, rice, sauce and 1 diced onion and bring to a boil.
2. Reduce the heat to low and simmer for about 20 minutes.
3. Meanwhile, heat tortillas in a large skillet till soft enough to fold.
4. Place the chicken onto each tortilla, followed by the shredded Jack cheese, diced onion, olives, rice mixture and beans. Roll the tortillas, tucking in sides to secure the filling.
5. In a large skillet, heat the oil and fry the filled tortillas, till browned from all sides.
6. Drain on paper towels.
7. In a medium bowl add the avocados, cilantro, lemon juice, green onions, chili peppers and tomatoes and mash to combine.
8. In a platter, place the shredded lettuce and top with the chimichangas, avocado mixture, sour cream and shredded Cheddar cheese.

I ♥ Latin Couscous

🍲 Prep Time: 15 mins
🕐 Total Time: 25 mins

Servings per Recipe: 4
Calories	300 kcal
Fat	10.9 g
Cholesterol	44.8g
Sodium	7.1 g
Carbohydrates	0 mg
Protein	713 mg

Ingredients

1 C. couscous
1/2 tsp ground cumin
1 tsp salt
1 1/4 C. boiling water
1 clove unpeeled garlic
1 (15 oz.) can black beans, rinsed and drained
1 C. canned whole kernel corn, drained

1/2 C. finely chopped red onion
1/4 C. chopped fresh cilantro
1 jalapeno pepper, minced
3 tbsp olive oil
3 tbsp fresh lime juice

Directions

1. In a large bowl, mix together the couscous, cumin and salt.
2. Add the boiling water and stir to combine.
3. Tightly, cover with a plastic wrap and keep aside for about 10 minutes.
4. Meanwhile in a small skillet, cook the unpeeled garlic clove on medium-high heat till toasted and the skin has turned golden-brown.
5. Peel the garlic clove and mince it. Add the minced garlic, the black beans, corn, onion, cilantro, jalapeño pepper, olive oil and lime juice in the bowl with couscous and mix. Serve warm or cold as well.

CLASSICAL
Hummus II (Red)

Prep Time: 15 mins
Total Time: 1 hr 15 mins

Servings per Recipe: 8

Calories	64 kcal
Fat	2.2 g
Carbohydrates	9.6g
Protein	2.5 g
Cholesterol	0 mg
Sodium	370 mg

Ingredients

1 (15 oz.) can garbanzo beans, drained
1 (4 oz.) jar roasted red peppers
3 tbsps lemon juice
1 1/2 tbsps tahini
1 clove garlic, minced
1/2 tsp ground cumin

1/2 tsp cayenne pepper
1/4 tsp salt
1 tbsp chopped fresh parsley

Directions

1. Blend the following until smooth: salt, chickpeas, cayenne, red peppers, cumin, lemon juice, garlic, and tahini.
2. Add everything to a bowl and place a covering of plastic over it.
3. Now place it all in the fridge for 60 mins.
4. Before serving the mix top the hummus with parsley.
5. Enjoy.

Greek Style
Macaroni Salad

Prep Time: 15 mins
Total Time: 2 hrs 25 mins

Servings per Recipe: 4
Calories	746 kcal
Fat	56.1 g
Carbohydrates	40.4g
Protein	22.1 g
Cholesterol	70 mg
Sodium	1279 mg

Ingredients

1/2 C. olive oil
1/2 C. apple cider vinegar
1 1/2 tsps garlic powder
1 1/2 tsps dried basil
1 1/2 tsps dried oregano
3/4 tsp ground black pepper
3/4 tsp white sugar
2 1/2 C. cooked elbow macaroni
3 C. fresh sliced mushrooms
15 cherry tomatoes, halved

1 C. sliced red bell peppers
3/4 C. crumbled feta cheese
1/2 C. chopped green onions
1 (4 oz.) can whole black olives
3/4 C. sliced beef sausage, cut into strips

Directions

1. Get a bowl, combine: sugar, pepperoni, olive oil, olives, pasta, black pepper, onions, feta, mushrooms, red peppers, tomatoes, vinegar, oregano, garlic powder, and basil.
2. Place a covering of plastic around the bowl and place everything in the fridge for 3 hrs.
3. Enjoy.

PITA, PESTO,
and Parmesan
(Greek Style Bake)

🍲 Prep Time: 10 mins

🕐 Total Time: 22 mins

Servings per Recipe: 6

Calories	350 kcal
Fat	17.1 g
Carbohydrates	41.6g
Protein	11.6 g
Cholesterol	13 mg
Sodium	587 mg

Ingredients

1 (6 oz.) tub sun-dried tomato pesto
6 (6 inch) whole wheat pita breads
2 roma (plum) tomatoes, chopped
1 bunch spinach, rinsed and chopped
4 fresh mushrooms, sliced
1/2 C. crumbled feta cheese

2 tbsps grated Parmesan cheese
3 tbsps olive oil
ground black pepper to taste

Directions

1. Set your oven to 350 degrees before doing anything else.
2. Coat each piece of pita with some pesto and then layer each with: pepper, tomatoes, olive oil, spinach, parmesan, mushrooms, and feta.
3. Cook the bread, for 15 mins, in the oven, and then cut them into triangles before serving.
4. Enjoy.

Mediterranean
Pasta

Prep Time: 20 mins
Total Time: 40 mins

Servings per Recipe: 4
Calories	685 kcal
Fat	13.2 g
Carbohydrates	96.2g
Protein	47 g
Cholesterol	94 mg
Sodium	826 mg

Ingredients

1 (16 oz.) package penne pasta
1 1/2 tbsps butter
1/2 C. chopped red onion
2 cloves garlic, minced
1 lb. skinless, boneless chicken breast halves - cut into bite-size pieces
1 (14 oz.) can artichoke hearts in water
1 tomato, chopped

1/2 C. crumbled feta cheese
3 tbsps chopped fresh parsley
2 tbsps lemon juice
1 tsp dried oregano
salt to taste
ground black pepper to taste

Directions

1. Boil your pasta in water and salt for 9 mins then remove all the liquids.
2. At the same time, stir fry your garlic and onions in butter for 4 mins, then combine in the chicken, and cook everything for 9 more mins.
3. Set the heat to a low level and add in your artichokes after chopping them and discarding their liquids.
4. Cook this mix for 3 more mins before adding in: pasta, tomatoes, oregano, feta, lemon juice, and the fresh parsley.
5. Cook everything for 4 mins to get it all hot. Then add in your pepper and salt after shutting the heat.
6. Enjoy.

GREEK
Burgers

Prep Time: 10 mins
Total Time: 40 mins

Servings per Recipe: 4

Calories	318 kcal
Fat	21.9 g
Carbohydrates	3.6g
Protein	25.5 g
Cholesterol	123 mg
Sodium	800 mg

Ingredients

1 lb. ground turkey
1 C. crumbled feta cheese
1/2 C. kalamata olives, pitted and sliced

2 tsps dried oregano
ground black pepper to taste

Directions

1. Get a bowl, combine: pepper, turkey, oregano, feta, and olives. Shape this into burgers and then grill each one for 6 mins.
2. Flip the patty and cook it for 7 more mins.
3. Enjoy.

Easiest
Greek Chicken

Prep Time: 10 mins

Total Time: 8 hrs 30 mins

Servings per Recipe: 4

Calories	644 kcal
Fat	57.6 g
Carbohydrates	4g
Protein	27.8 g
Cholesterol	68 mg
Sodium	660 mg

Ingredients

4 skinless, boneless chicken breast halves
1 C. extra virgin olive oil
1 lemon, juiced
2 tsps crushed garlic

1 tsp salt
1 1/2 tsps black pepper
1/3 tsp paprika

Directions

1. Slice a few incisions into your pieces of chicken before doing anything else.
2. Now get a bowl, combine: paprika, olive oil, pepper, lemon juice, salt, and garlic.
3. Now add in the chicken and place the contents in the fridge for 8 hrs.
4. Grill your chicken until fully done with indirect heat on the side of the grill with the grilling grates oiled.
5. Enjoy..

GREEK
Falafel

Prep Time: 25 mins
Total Time: 32 mins

Servings per Recipe: 6

Calories	317 kcal
Fat	16.8 g
Carbohydrates	35.2g
Protein	7.2 g
Cholesterol	0 mg
Sodium	724 mg

Ingredients

1 (19 oz.) can garbanzo beans, rinsed and drained
1 small onion, finely chopped
2 cloves garlic, minced
1 1/2 tbsps chopped fresh cilantro
1 tsp dried parsley
2 tsps ground cumin
1/8 tsp ground turmeric
1/2 tsp baking powder
1 C. fine dry bread crumbs
3/4 tsp salt
1/4 tsp cracked black peppercorns
1 quart vegetable oil for frying

Directions

1. Get a bowl, combine: pepper, onions, salt, garlic, bread crumbs, cilantro, baking powder, parsley, mashed garbanzos, turmeric, and cumin.
2. Form the contents into small balls and make about 20 of them.
3. Deep fry these falafels in hot oil until golden.
4. Enjoy.

Chicken
Souvlaki

Prep Time: 15 mins

Total Time: 2 hrs 30 mins

Servings per Recipe: 6
Calories	268 kcal
Fat	16.8 g
Carbohydrates	2.6g
Protein	< 25.5 g
Cholesterol	71 mg
Sodium	295 mg

Ingredients

1/4 C. olive oil
2 tbsps lemon juice
2 cloves garlic, minced
1 tsp dried oregano
1/2 tsp salt
1 1/2 lbs skinless, boneless chicken breast halves - cut into bite-sized pieces
Sauce:
1 (6 oz.) container plain Greek-style yogurt

1/2 cucumber - peeled, seeded, and grated
1 tbsp olive oil
2 tsps white vinegar
1 clove garlic, minced
1 pinch salt
6 wooden skewers, or as needed

Directions

1. Take your skewers and submerge them in water before doing anything else.
2. Get a bowl, mix: half tsp salt, quarter of a C. of olive oil, chicken, oregano, lemon juice, and 2 cloves of garlic.
3. Place a covering on the bowl and put it all in the fridge for 3 hrs.
4. Get a 2nd bowl, combine: some salt, yogurt, 1 piece of garlic, 1 tbsp of olive oil, and the cucumbers.
5. Place this in the fridge for 3 hrs as well.
6. Stake your chicken on the skewers and then grill them for 9 mins, turn them over and cook for 8 more mins.
7. Top the chicken with the white sauce.
8. Enjoy.

CHICKEN WONTONS
with Homemade Duck Sauce

Prep Time: 30 mins
Total Time: 30 mins

Servings per Recipe: 1
Calories	120.5
Fat	3.5g
Cholesterol	10.0mg
Sodium	443.4mg
Carbohydrates	17.5g
Protein	4.7g

Ingredients

Marinade:
3 tsp brown sugar
2 tsp salt
4 garlic cloves, minced
4 tsp dry sherry
2 tsp cornstarch
6 tbsp vegetable oil
1 tsp soy sauce
1 lb boneless skinless chicken breast, diced
Wrappers
1 (12 oz.) packages wonton wrappers (the smaller 3 1/2 -inch square ones)
peanut oil, for frying (about 2 C.)
Duck Sauce
12 oz. apricot preserves
4 tsp yellow mustard
4 tbsp teriyaki sauce

Directions

1. For the chicken marinade, in a large bowl, mix together all the ingredients except the chicken. Add the chicken pieces and coat them with the mixture generously and refrigerate, covered for about 8 hours to overnight.
2. Place 1 piece of chicken, followed by 1 dash of marinade in the center of each wonton wrapper. Coat the edges of the wrappers with wet fingers and fold them over the filling in a square envelope.
3. With your fingers, press the edges to seal them completely.
4. In a large skillet heat the oil to 375 degrees F.
5. Add the wontons in batches and cook them for about 2 minutes on both sides.
6. Transfer the wrappers onto a paper towel lined plate to drain.
7. For the sauce, in a bowl, mix together all the sauce ingredients.
8. Serve the wontons alongside the sauce.

Loaded
Asiago Wontons

Prep Time: 25 mins
Total Time: 40 mins

Servings per Recipe: 1	
Calories	50.1
Fat	2.0g
Cholesterol	5.9mg
Sodium	70.5mg
Carbohydrates	6.5g
Protein	1.5g

Ingredients

1/2 tbsp olive oil
1/4 C. onion, finely chopped
1/4 C. shallot, minced
1 garlic clove, minced
4 oz. cream cheese, softened
1/4 C. mayonnaise
7 oz. quartered artichoke hearts in brine
1/8 tsp ground cayenne pepper

5 oz. frozen chopped spinach, thawed and squeezed dry
1/4 C. grated Asiago cheese
salt
24 wonton wrappers
water
cooking spray

Directions

1. Set your oven to 375 degrees F before doing anything else and arrange the rack in the upper third part of the oven.
2. Lightly, grease a baking sheet.
3. In a large skillet, heat the oil on medium heat and sauté the shallots and onion for about 2 minutes.
4. Stir in the garlic and sauté for about 30 seconds and remove from the heat.
5. In a food processor, add the artichoke hearts, mayonnaise, cream cheese and cayenne pepper and pulse till smooth.
6. In a bowl, add the artichoke mixture, onion mixture, spinach, Asiago cheese and salt and mix till well combined.
7. Place about 1/2 tsp of the chocolate chips, followed by 1 strawberry piece in the center of each wonton wrapper.
8. Coat the edges of the wrappers with wet fingers and fold them over the filling in a triangle shape.

9. With your fingers, press the edges to seal them completely.
10. Arrange the wontons onto the prepared baking sheet and cook everything in the oven for about 10 minutes.
11. Carefully, flip the side and cook everything in the oven for about 4 minutes..

Pinto Beans
from Texas

Prep Time: 15 mins
Total Time: 2 hrs 15 mins

Servings per Recipe: 8
Calories	210 kcal
Fat	1.1 g
Carbohydrates	37.9 g
Protein	13.2 g
Cholesterol	1 mg
Sodium	< 95 mg

Ingredients

1 lb dry pinto beans
1 (29 oz.) can reduced sodium chicken broth
1 large onion, diced
1 fresh jalapeno pepper, diced
2 cloves garlic, minced
1/2 C. green salsa

1 tsp cumin
1/2 tsp ground black pepper
water, if needed

Directions

1. Get the following boiling: pepper, beans, cumin, broth, onions, salsa, jalapenos, and garlic.
2. Let the contents cook for 2 hrs.
3. If the mix gets too dry add some water and continue cooking for the remaining time.
4. Enjoy.

EASY JALAPENO
Bites

🥄 Prep Time: 1 hr
🕐 Total Time: 1 hr 20 mins

Servings per Recipe: 20
Calories	189 kcal
Fat	18.2 g
Carbohydrates	2g
Protein	< 4.6 g
Cholesterol	40 mg
Sodium	256 mg

Ingredients

2 (12 oz.) packages ground beef sausage
2 (8 oz.) packages cream cheese, softened
30 jalapeno chili peppers, cut in half horizontally,
seeds taken out

1 lb sliced turkey bacon, cut in half

Directions

1. Set your oven to 375 degrees before doing anything else.
2. Stir fry your sausage until fully done then place them in a bowl with the cream cheese.
3. Fill your pieces of pepper with the sausage mix and then wrap bacon around each one.
4. Place the contents into a casserole dish and cook everything in the oven for 24 mins.
5. Enjoy.

Texas Style
Fried Chicken

Prep Time: 30 mins
Total Time: 6 hrs 50 mins

Servings per Recipe: 4
Calories	666 kcal
Fat	21.3 g
Carbohydrates	85.6g
Protein	32.7 g
Cholesterol	140 mg
Sodium	1151 mg

Ingredients

2 C. buttermilk
1 tsp onion powder
1/4 C. diced fresh parsley
1/4 C. diced fresh tarragon
1/4 C. diced fresh sage
1 tsp paprika
1 tsp ground cayenne pepper
2 skinless, boneless chicken breast halves, halved
2 C. all-purpose flour
1 tsp garlic salt
1 tsp onion salt
1 tsp ground cayenne pepper

salt and ground black pepper to taste
2 eggs
2 tbsps whole milk
ground black pepper to taste
2 C. grapeseed oil for frying
1/2 C. all-purpose flour
1/2 C. quick-mixing flour (such as Wondra(R))
2 C. whole milk
1 pinch salt and ground white pepper to taste

Directions

1.   Get a bowl, combine: 1 tsp cayenne, buttermilk, paprika, onion powder, sage, parsley, and tarragon.
2.   Add in your chicken to the mix and coat the pieces evenly.
3.   Place a covering of plastic on the bowl and put everything in the fridge overnight.
4.   Get a 2nd bowl, mix: black pepper, 2 C. flour, salt, garlic salt, 1 tsp cayenne, and onion salt.
5.   Get a 3rd bowl, whisk: 2 tbsps milk, eggs, pepper, and salt.
6.   Get a 4rd bowl and add in 1/2 C. of flour without any spices.
7.   Dredge your chicken first in the 4th bowl, then the 3rd bowl, and finally the 2nd.

8. For 10 mins, per side, fry your chicken in grapeseed oil then place on a rack.
9. Leave a quarter of a C. of oil in the pan and begin adding the quick mix flour and milk to the oil while stirring.
10. Get the mixing gently boiling and continue stirring until the gravy is thick.
11. Now add some pepper and salt and top the chicken pieces with it.
12. Enjoy.

Sweet Honey
Chicken

Prep Time: 10 mins

Total Time: 1 hr 45 mins

Servings per Recipe: 4

Calories	481 kcal
Fat	21.5 g
Carbohydrates	49.4g
Protein	22.8 g
Cholesterol	65 mg
Sodium	6378 mg

Ingredients

3 C. cold water
1/4 C. kosher salt
1/4 C. honey
4 boneless skinless chicken breast halves
1/4 C. buttermilk
1 C. all-purpose flour
1 tsp black pepper

1/2 tsp garlic salt
1/2 tsp onion salt
cayenne pepper to taste
vegetable oil for frying

Directions

1. Get a bowl, combine: honey, water, and salt.
2. Now place the chicken in the water (make sure the liquid covers the chicken).
3. Place a covering of plastic wrap around the bowl and chill the mix in the fridge for 2 hrs.
4. Now put your chicken in another bowl and cover it with buttermilk.
5. Let the chicken stand for 30 mins in the milk.
6. Add your veggie oil to a frying and pan and begin heating it to 350 degrees before doing anything else.
7. Now get a 3rd bowl, mix: cayenne, flour, onion salt, garlic salt, and black pepper.
8. Dredge your chicken in the dry mix then fry it for 13 mins per side in the hot oil
9. Enjoy.

TEXAS MEXICAN
Burritos

Prep Time: 15 mins
Total Time: 45 mins

Servings per Recipe: 6
Calories	916 kcal
Fat	42 g
Carbohydrates	92g
Protein	43.9 g
Cholesterol	122 mg
Sodium	2285 mg

Ingredients

1 lb ground beef
1/2 C. diced onion
1 clove garlic, minced
1/2 tsp cumin
1/4 tsp salt
1/8 tsp pepper
1 (4.5 oz.) can diced green chili peppers
1 (16 oz.) can refried beans
1 (15 oz.) can chili without beans

1 (10.75 oz.) can condensed tomato soup
1 (10 oz.) can enchilada sauce
6 (12 inch) flour tortillas, warmed
2 C. shredded lettuce
1 C. diced tomatoes
2 C. shredded Mexican blend cheese
1/2 C. diced green onions

Directions

1. Stir fry and crumble your beef in a frying pan until it is fully done.
2. Then add in the onions and continue frying the onions until they are see-through.
3. Remove the excess oil and add: pepper, beans, garlic, green chilies, salt, and cumin.
4. Get all the contents hot and then shut the heat.
5. Now in another big pot heat the following: enchilada sauce, chili without beans, and tomato soup.
6. Add half a C. of beef to a tortilla, and add some tomato and lettuce.
7. Form an enchilada by rolling the tortilla.
8. Now add a liberal amount of tomato mix over the enchilada and a topping of green onions and cheese. For 40 secs heat the enchilada in the microwave.
9. Continue for the rest of the ingredients. Enjoy.

Carolina
Sweet Chicken

🥣 Prep Time: 10 mins

🕐 Total Time: 8 hrs 50 mins

Servings per Recipe: 10

Calories	877 kcal
Fat	68.5 g
Carbohydrates	120.4g
Protein	44 g
Cholesterol	222 mg
Sodium	1137 mg

Ingredients

4 eggs
1/4 C. cornstarch
1/4 C. white sugar
5 cloves garlic, minced
1/2 C. sweet rice flour
4 tsp salt
4 green onions, chopped

1/4 C. oyster sauce
5 lb. boneless chicken thighs, cut in half
2 C. vegetable oil, for deep frying

Directions

1. In a large bowl, mix together all the ingredients except the chicken and oil.
2. Add the chicken pieces and coat them with the mixture generously.
3. Cover and refrigerate everything to marinate overnight.
4. Remove the chicken pieces from the refrigerator and keep everything aside in at room temperature for about 10 minutes before cooking.
5. In a large skillet, heat the oil to 375 degrees F and fry the chicken pieces till golden brown completely.
6. Transfer the chicken pieces onto paper towel lined plates to drain.

AUTHENTIC
Southern Corn

🥣 Prep Time: 10 mins

🕐 Total Time: 20 mins

Servings per Recipe: 6
Calories	359 kcal
Fat	22.7 g
Carbohydrates	38.2g
Protein	8 g
Cholesterol	61 mg
Sodium	491 mg

Ingredients

2 (15.25 oz.) cans whole kernel corn, drained
1 (8 oz.) package cream cheese
1/4 C. butter
10 jalapeno peppers, diced

1 tsp garlic salt

Directions

1. Cook the following for 15 mins, in a large, pot: garlic salt, corn, jalapenos, butter, and cream cheese.
2. Stir the mix every 2 to 3 mins.
3. Enjoy.

Buttermilk
Paprika Fried Chicken

Prep Time: 30 mins
Total Time: 50 mins

Servings per Recipe: 8
Calories	489 kcal
Fat	21.8 g
Carbohydrates	29.5g
Protein	40.7 g
Cholesterol	116 mg
Sodium	140 mg

Ingredients

1 (4 lb.) chicken, cut into pieces
1 C. buttermilk
2 C. all-purpose flour for coating
1 tsp paprika

salt and pepper to taste
2 quarts vegetable oil for frying

Directions

1. In a shallow dish, place the buttermilk.
2. In another shallow dish, place the flour, salt, black pepper and paprika.
3. Dip the chicken pieces in the buttermilk completely and coat them in the flour mixture.
4. Arrange the chicken pieces on a baking dish and cover with wax paper and keep aside till flour becomes pasty.
5. In a large cast iron skillet, heat the vegetable oil and fry the chicken pieces till browned.
6. Reduce the heat and cook, covered for about 30 minutes.
7. Uncover and increase the heat and cook till crispy.
8. Transfer the chicken pieces onto paper towel lined plates to drain.

SOUTHERN LOUISIANA
Vegetable Medley (Maque Choux)

Prep Time: 35 mins
Total Time: 1 hr 5 mins

Servings per Recipe: 6

Calories	211 kcal
Fat	11.1 g
Carbohydrates	22.8g
Protein	8.6 g
Cholesterol	14 mg
Sodium	371 mg

Ingredients

6 ears corn, husked and cleaned
2 tbsps vegetable oil
1 large onion, thinly sliced
1 C. green bell pepper, chopped
1 large fresh tomato, chopped
1/4 C. milk

salt to taste
cayenne pepper
1/4 C. chopped green onions
8 strips crisply cooked turkey bacon, crumbled

Directions

1. Get a bowl.
2. With a sharp knife, safely slice the kernels of corn off of the cob. Add the milk to the bowl and stir everything.
3. Begin to stir fry your green pepper and onions, in oil, for 7 mins, then add in the tomatoes and corn.
4. Set the heat to low and let the mix cook for 25 mins.
5. Stir the mix every 5 mins but avoid boiling it.
6. Then add in the cayenne and salt.
7. Stir the spices in evenly then set the heat lower, place a lid on the pan, and continue cooking everything for 7 more mins.
8. Now add your bacon and the green onions.
9. Enjoy.

Tex Mex Shrimp

🥣 Prep Time: 20 mins
🕐 Total Time: 20 mins

Servings per Recipe: 8
Calories	76 kcal
Fat	0.8 g
Carbohydrates	4.8g
Protein	12.9 g
Cholesterol	111 mg
Sodium	279 mg

Ingredients

1 lb cooked medium shrimp, chilled
1/2 large cucumber, cut into 1/2 inch cubes
1/2 large tomato, cut into 1/2 inch cubes
8 green onions, thinly sliced
1 oz. fresh cilantro, finely diced
1 serrano pepper, thinly sliced

1 (8 oz.) can tomato sauce
2 tbsps white vinegar
1 lime

Directions

1. Get a bowl, combine: vinegar, shrimp, tomato sauce, cucumber, serrano, green onions, and cilantro.
2. Top this mix with the lime and place it in the fridge until chilled.
3. Enjoy.

SOUTHERN MACARONI
and Cheese

🥣 Prep Time: 10 mins

🕐 Total Time: 1 hr 5 mins

Servings per Recipe: 6
Calories	561 kcal
Fat	33.3 g
Carbohydrates	36.5g
Protein	28.3 g
Cholesterol	100 mg
Sodium	1194 mg

Ingredients

2 tbsps butter
1/4 C. finely diced onion
2 tbsps all-purpose flour
2 C. milk
3/4 tsp salt
1/2 tsp dry mustard

1/4 tsp ground black pepper
1 (8 oz.) package elbow macaroni
2 C. shredded sharp Cheddar cheese
1 (8 oz.) package processed American cheese, cut into strips

Directions

1. Set your oven to 350 degrees before doing anything else.
2. Boil your pasta for 9 mins in water and salt. Then remove all the liquids.
3. Stir fry your onions in butter for 4 mins then add the flour and cook the mix for 20 more secs while mixing.
4. Now add in: pepper, milk, mustard, and salt.
5. Continue to heat and stir, until everything starts boiling and becomes thick.
6. Once the sauce has become thick add in the cheese and cook the sauce until the cheese melts, while continuing to stir.
7. Add the pasta to the sauce, stir the mix once, and then pour everything into a casserole dish.
8. Cook the contents in the oven for 35 mins.
9. Enjoy.

Authentic
New England Style Clam Chowder

Prep Time: 15 mins
Total Time: 45 mins

Servings per Recipe: 8
Calories	396 kcal
Fat	22.5 g
Carbohydrates	24g
Protein	24.1 g
Cholesterol	101 mg
Sodium	706 mg

Ingredients

4 turkey bacon slices, chopped
1 1/2 C. onion, chopped
4 C. potatoes, peeled and cubed
1 1/2 C. water
Salt and freshly ground black pepper, to taste
3 tbsps butter

3 C. half-and-half
2 (10-oz.) cans minced clams, drained, reserving 1/2 C. of liquid

Directions

1. Heat a large nonstick soup pan on medium-high heat.
2. Add the bacon and cook for about 8-10 minutes.
3. Transfer the bacon into a bowl, leaving the fats in pan.
4. Add the onion and sauté for about 4-5 minutes with medium heat.
5. Add the potatoes and water and bring to a boil.
6. Cook, uncovered for about 15 minutes or till tender enough.
7. Stir in the butter and half-and-half.
8. Add clams with reserved liquid and stir to combine.
9. Cook, stirring occasionally, for about 5 minutes.
10. Serve hot with a topping of bacon.

NEW ENGLAND
Fried Chips and Fried Fish

Prep Time: 10 mins
Total Time: 45 mins

Servings per Recipe: 4
Calories	782 kcal
Fat	26.2 g
Carbohydrates	91.9g
Protein	44.6 g
Cholesterol	125 mg
Sodium	861 mg

Ingredients

1 C. all-purpose flour
1 tsp baking powder
Salt and freshly ground black pepper, to taste
1 egg, beaten lightly
1 C. milk
4 large potatoes, peeled and cut into strips lengthwise

4 C. vegetable oil
1 1/2 lbs cod fillets

Directions

1. In a large bowl, add flour, baking powder, salt, black pepper, egg and milk.
2. Mix till well combined.
3. Keep everything aside for at least 20 minutes.
4. In a large bowl of chilled water, dip the potatoes for 2-3 minutes.
5. Drain the mix well and pat dry with paper towel.
6. In a large skillet, heat the oil with medium heat.
7. Add the potatoes and fry for about 3-4 minutes or till crisp and tender.
8. Transfer the potatoes onto a paper towel lined plate.
9. Coat the cod fillets in the flour mixture evenly.
10. Fry everything for about 3-4 minutes or till golden brown.
11. Transfer the cod fillets onto another paper towel lined plate.
12. Now, return the potato strips to the skillet and fry them for about 1-2 minutes more or till crispy.

Fettuccini
Shrimp & Scallions

🥣 Prep Time: 15 mins
🕐 Total Time: 35 mins

Servings per Recipe: 6
Calories	662 kcal
Fat	29.5 g
Carbohydrates	61g
Protein	29.3 g
Cholesterol	162 mg
Sodium	1109 mg

Ingredients

1 (16-oz.) package dry fettuccini noodles
1/4 C. olive oil
1 lb shrimp, peeled and deveined
1/4 C. grape juice
6 scallions, sliced thinly
4 garlic cloves, sliced thinly
2 large tomatoes, chopped

1/2 C. butter
1/2 C. broth
1/2 C. fresh basil, chopped
Salt and freshly ground black pepper, to taste
1/2 C. parmesan cheese, grated

Directions

1. In a large pan of lightly salted boiling water, add the noodles and cook them for about 8-10 minutes.
2. Drain well and keep aside.
3. In a large skillet, heat the oil with medium heat.
4. Add the shrimp and cook them for about 1-2 minutes.
5. Stir in the grape juice, scallions and garlic.
6. With a gas flame or match carefully, ignite the brandy.
7. Cook everything for about 2 minutes.
8. Stir in the tomatoes and cook them for about 2 minutes.
9. Add the butter, broth and basil and stir to combine.
10. Continue cooking everything for about 3 minutes.
11. Stir in the cheese till combined.
12. Add the noodles and toss to coat. Serve the dish hot.

YANKEE
Fried Honey and Garlic Chicken

Prep Time: 30 mins

Total Time: 1 hr 10 mins

Servings per Recipe: 8

Calories	566 kcal
Fat	28.5 g
Carbohydrates	42.2g
Protein	34.2 g
Cholesterol	97 mg
Sodium	234 mg

Ingredients

1 (4-lb) whole chicken, cut into 8 pieces
Salt and freshly ground black pepper, to taste
1/2 C. honey
2 C. all-purpose flour
1 package chicken bouillon granules

1 tbsp garlic powder
4 C. vegetable oil

Directions

1. In a large bowl, place the chicken.
2. Sprinkle the pieces with salt and black pepper generously.
3. Add the honey and toss to coat.
4. In a large shallow dish, add the flour, bouillon granules and garlic powder and mix.
5. Now, roll the chicken pieces in the flour mixture evenly.
6. In a large skillet, heat the oil on medium-high heat.
7. Add the chicken and fry them for about 5 minutes on both sides or till desired doneness.

Manhattan
Style Cheesecake

Prep Time: 40 mins
Total Time: 7 hrs 35 mins

Servings per Recipe: 12
Calories	509 kcal
Fat	35.4 g
Carbohydrates	40.8g
Protein	8.3 g
Cholesterol	154 mg
Sodium	310 mg

Ingredients

1 1/2 C. graham cracker crumbs
1/4 C. white sugar
1/3 C. butter, melted
3 (8 oz.) packages cream cheese, room temperature
4 eggs, room temperature
1 tbsp vanilla extract
1 C. white sugar

1 tsp cream of tartar
1 pint sour cream
1 tsp vanilla extract
1/2 C. white sugar

Directions

1. Set your oven to 350 degrees before doing anything else.
2. Get a bowl, combine: butter, cracker crumbs, and sugar.
3. Layer the crumb mix into the bottom of a spring form pan and also half an inch along the sides of the pan as well.
4. Get a 2nd bowl, mix with an electric mixer: sugar and cream cheese.
5. Once the mix is light and fluffy add in the cream of tartar, 1 tbsp vanilla, and eggs.
6. Combine the mix again until it is smooth then enter everything into the pan as well.
7. Cook the cheesecake in the oven for 55 mins.
8. Get a 3rd bowl, combine: 1/2 C. sugar, 1 tsp vanilla, and sour cream.
9. Top your cake with the mix evenly then place everything in the oven again for 7 more mins.
10. Enjoy.

CLASSICAL
Baked Beans from Boston

Prep Time: 30 mins
Total Time: 5 hrs

Servings per Recipe: 6
Calories	382 kcal
Fat	6.3 g
Carbohydrates	63.1g
Protein	20.7 g
Cholesterol	14 mg
Sodium	1320 mg

Ingredients

2 C. navy beans, soaked in a large bowl of water for overnight
1 onion, chopped finely
1/2 lb turkey bacon, chopped
1/2 C. ketchup
1/4 C. brown sugar

3 tbsps molasses
1 tbsp Worcestershire sauce
1/4 tsp dry mustard
Salt and freshly ground black pepper, to taste

Directions

1. In a large pan, add the beans and soaked water.
2. Get everything boiling on high heat. Reduce the heat to medium-low.
3. Cover and simmer for about 1-2 hours or till tender enough. Drain well and reserve the liquid into a bowl. Now preheat the oven 325 degrees F.
4. In a bowl, mix together the onion and bacon.
5. Place the beans in the bottom of a casserole dish.
6. Place the bacon mixture over the beans evenly.
7. In a pan, mix together the remaining ingredients with medium heat.
8. Bring to a boil, stirring continuously. Place the molasses mixture over the beans evenly.
9. Place enough reserved cooking liquid to cover the beans.
10. With a lid, cover, the casserole dish.
11. Bake everything for about 3-4 hours.
12. Half way through cooking uncover the casserole dish.

Authentic
Eggplant Parmesan

🍲 Prep Time: 25 mins

🕐 Total Time: 1 hr

Servings per Recipe: 10

Calories	487 kcal
Fat	16 g
Carbohydrates	62.1g
Protein	24.2 g
Cholesterol	73 mg
Sodium	1663 mg

Ingredients

3 eggplant, peeled and thinly sliced
2 eggs, beaten
4 C. Italian seasoned bread crumbs
6 C. spaghetti sauce, divided
1 (16 oz.) package mozzarella cheese, shredded and divided

1/2 C. grated Parmesan cheese, divided
1/2 tsp dried basil

Directions

1. Set your oven to 350 degrees before doing anything else.
2. Coat your pieces of eggplant with egg then with bread crumbs.
3. Now lay the veggies on a cookie sheet and cook them in the oven for 6 mins. Flip the eggplants and cook them for 6 more mins.
4. Coat the bottom of a casserole dish with pasta sauce then layer some of your eggplants in the dish.
5. Top the veggies with some parmesan and mozzarella then layer your eggplants, sauce, and cheese.
6. Continue this pattern until all the ingredients have been used up.
7. Finally coat the layer with some basil and cook everything in the oven for 40 mins. Enjoy.

AUTHENTIC
Meatball Sub

Prep Time: 15 mins
Total Time: 1 hr 40 mins

Servings per Recipe: 6
Calories   491 kcal
Fat   21.4 g
Carbohydrates   43.1g
Protein   29.3 g
Cholesterol   75 mg
Sodium   1068 mg

Ingredients

1 1/2 lbs lean ground beef
1/3 C. Italian seasoned bread crumbs
1/2 small onion, diced
1 tsp salt
1/2 C. shredded mozzarella cheese, divided

1 tbsp cracked black pepper
1 tsp garlic powder
1/2 C. marinara sauce
3 hoagie rolls, split lengthwise

Directions

1. Set your oven to 350 degrees before doing anything else.
2. Get a bowl, combine: 1/2 of the mozzarella, beef, garlic powder, bread crumbs, pepper, onions, and salt. Shape the mix into a large loaf then place it in a casserole dish. Cook the meat in the oven for 55 mins then let it cool for 10 mins. Cut the meat into slices then layer the pieces of meat on a roll. Top everything with the marinara then add a topping of cheese. Cover the sandwich with some foil and put everything in the oven for 20 more mins.
3. Let the sandwich cool for 20 mins then cut each one in half.
4. Enjoy.

Italian Pepper and Pasta (Riggies) (Utica, NY Style)

Prep Time: 25 mins
Total Time: 45 mins

Servings per Recipe: 6

Calories	613 kcal
Fat	20.7 g
Carbohydrates	70.8g
Protein	38.2 g
Cholesterol	92 mg
Sodium	576 mg

Ingredients

1 (16 oz.) package rigatoni pasta
3 tbsps extra-virgin olive oil
1 1/2 lbs skinless, boneless chicken breast, cut in bite-sized pieces
salt and pepper to taste
1 onion, diced
3 cloves garlic, minced
2 cubanelle pepper, seeded and thinly sliced

3 roasted red peppers, drained and chopped
2 hot cherry peppers, seeded and minced
1 (28 oz.) can crushed tomatoes
1/2 C. heavy cream
1/2 C. grated Parmesan cheese

Directions

1. Get your pasta boiling in water and salt for 9 mins then remove all the liquids.
2. Top your chicken with some pepper and salt then fry it in olive oil for 8 mins until it is fully done and browned all over.
3. Place the chicken to the side. Then add in the cubanelle pepper, garlic and onions.
4. Cook the mix for 5 mins then add in the crushed tomatoes, cherry pepper, and roast peppers.
5. Get everything simmering then add the cream and the chicken.
6. Let the mix cook for 5 mins then add the pasta and toss everything together.
7. When serving the dish coat it with parmesan cheese.
8. Enjoy.

DIJON
Downstate Chicken

Prep Time: 20 mins
Total Time: 30 mins

Servings per Recipe: 8
Calories	486 kcal
Fat	33.1 g
Carbohydrates	15.5g
Protein	28.6 g
Cholesterol	134 mg
Sodium	537 mg

Ingredients

1/2 C. finely chopped pecans
1/2 C. dry bread crumbs
8 skinless, boneless chicken breast halves
1/4 C. clarified butter, melted
1/4 C. Dijon mustard
1/4 C. dark brown sugar
2 2/3 tbsps bourbon whiskey

2 tbsps soy sauce
1 tsp Worcestershire sauce
3/4 C. unsalted butter, chilled and cut into small cubes
1/2 C. sliced green onions

Directions

1. Get a bowl, combine: 2 tbsps clarified butter, bread crumbs, and pecans.
2. Dredge your chicken in this mix then add the rest of the butter to a skillet.
3. Fry your chicken for 11 mins each side.
4. Now get a small pot, heat and stir the following: Worcestershire, Dijon, soy sauce, brown sugar, and bourbon.
5. Get the mix boiling then shut the heat.
6. Add in 3/4 C. of unsalted butter slowly piece by piece. Top your chicken liberally with the bourbon sauce when serving. Enjoy.

Manhattan Island
Burgers

Prep Time: 25 mins
Total Time: 35 mins

Servings per Recipe: 8
Calories	336 kcal
Fat	17.5 g
Carbohydrates	29 g
Protein	15.4 g
Cholesterol	71 mg
Sodium	282 mg

Ingredients

1 lb ground beef
4 soft sun-dried tomatoes, chopped
2 green onions, finely chopped
2 cloves garlic, minced
1/2 green bell pepper, chopped
1 egg
3 tbsps bread crumbs
1 dash Worcestershire sauce

1 dash hot pepper sauce
salt and pepper to taste
1 tsp vegetable oil
8 English muffins, split and toasted

Directions

1. Get a bowl, combine: pepper, beef, salt, sun dried tomato, Worcestershire sauce, green onions, bread crumbs, garlic, egg, and bell peppers.
2. Work the mix with your hands then shape everything into 8 patties.
3. Now begin to fry your burgers in veggie oil for 7 mins each side.
4. Serve the burgers on English muffins that have been toasted.
5. Enjoy.

DOWNSTATE
Deli Coleslaw

🥣 Prep Time: 15 mins
🕐 Total Time: 15 mins

Servings per Recipe: 1
Calories   134.1
Cholesterol   5.0mg
Sodium   185.4mg
Carbohydrates   17.9g
Protein   2.6g

Ingredients

6 C. green cabbage, cored, shredded
6 C. red cabbage, cored, shredded
salt
2 tsps caraway seeds
1/2 C. mayonnaise
2 tbsps white vinegar
1 tsp dijon-style mustard

1 tsp sugar
pepper
2 carrots, peeled and grated
1 small sweet onion, minced

Directions

1. Place your cabbage in a colander and coat the leaves with 1 tsp of salt.
2. Let the leaves sit for 2 hours.
3. At the same time toast your caraways seeds for 5 mins in a skillet.
4. Now dry the cabbage with some paper towel and squeeze out any excess liquids.
5. Get a bowl, combine: 1/4 tsp pepper, caraway seeds, sugar, mayo, mustard, and vinegar.
6. Add in the onions, carrots, and cabbage and stir the mix.
7. Place a covering of plastic on the bowl and put everything in the fridge for 60 mins.
8. Top the coleslaw with some more pepper and salt then serve.
9. Enjoy.

Thai Style
Noodles

🥣 Prep Time: 30 mins
🕐 Total Time: 1 hr 5 mins

Servings per Recipe: 6
Calories	695 kcal
Fat	32.9 g
Carbohydrates	70.5g
Protein	35.3 g
Cholesterol	187 mg
Sodium	383 mg

Ingredients

4 eggs
1 tbsp soy sauce
1 tbsp sesame oil
canola oil
1 (12 oz.) package extra-firm tofu, cubed
2 C. sliced fresh mushrooms
2 C. broccoli florets
1/4 C. chopped cashews

1 (10 oz.) package frozen shelled edamame (green soybeans)
1 (16 oz.) package egg noodles
1/2 C. unsweetened soy milk
1/2 C. peanut butter
1/4 C. reduced-fat coconut milk
1 tsp tahini

Directions

1. Set your oven to 350 degrees F before doing anything else.
2. In a bowl, mix together the soy sauce and eggs.
3. Heat a nonstick skillet on medium heat and cook the egg mixture for about 3-5 minutes.
4. Transfer the cooked eggs onto a cutting board and chop them.
5. In a large skillet, heat both the oils on medium heat and cook the tofu for about 8-10 minutes.
6. Transfer the tofu into a bowl.
7. In the same skillet, add the broccoli and mushrooms and cook for about 5-7 minutes.
8. In a baking dish, place the cashews and cook them in the oven for about 8-12 minutes.
9. In a microwave safe bowl, place the edamame and microwave it, covered for about 1-2 minutes.
10. In a large pan of lightly salted boiling water, cook the egg noodles for about 8 minutes.
11. Drain them well and keep everything aside.

12. In a large pan, mix together the remaining ingredients on medium heat and cook, stirring continuously, for about 2-4 minutes.

13. Add the noodles, tofu, chopped eggs, edamame and broccoli mixture and toss to combine.

14. Serve with a topping of roasted cashews.

Hearty
Chili Noodles Bake

🥣 Prep Time: 15 mins
🕐 Total Time: 50 mins

Servings per Recipe: 6
Calories	510 kcal
Fat	20 g
Carbohydrates	49 g
Protein	27.6 g
Cholesterol	111 mg
Sodium	1129 mg

Ingredients

1 (12 oz.) package wide egg noodles
1 lb. ground beef
1 onion, chopped
3 cloves garlic, minced
2 (15 oz.) cans tomato sauce
1 (8 oz.) can tomato sauce
15 fluid oz. water
1 C. broth

1 tbsp ground cumin
1 tsp dried oregano
1/2 tsp cayenne pepper
1 C. shredded sharp Cheddar cheese

Directions

1. Set your oven to 350 degrees F before doing anything else and grease a 14x9-inch baking dish.
2. In a large pan of lightly salted boiling water, cook the egg noodles for about 5 minutes, stirring occasionally.
3. Drain them well and keep everything aside.
4. Heat a large skillet on medium-high heat and cook the beef till browned completely.
5. Add the onion and garlic and stir fry them till the onion becomes tender.
6. Add the tomato sauce, broth, water, oregano, cumin and cayenne pepper and bring to a simmer.
7. Stir in the pasta and place the mixture into the prepared baking dish.
8. Top everything with the cheddar cheese and cook everything in the oven for about 20 minutes.

NOODLES
& Shrimp Asian Style

🥣 Prep Time: 20 mins
🕐 Total Time: 30 mins

Servings per Recipe: 6
Calories	322 kcal
Fat	6.3 g
Carbohydrates	49 g
Protein	15.1 g
Cholesterol	83 mg
Sodium	616 mg

Ingredients

1 lb. fresh Chinese egg noodles
2 tbsp olive oil
1/3 C. chopped onion
1 clove garlic, chopped
3/4 C. broccoli florets
1/2 C. chopped red bell pepper
2 C. cooked shrimp

1/2 C. sliced water chestnuts, drained
1/2 C. baby corn, drained
1/2 C. canned sliced bamboo shoots, drained
3 tbsp oyster sauce
1 tbsp red pepper flakes, or to taste

Directions

1. In a large pan of lightly salted boiling water, cook the egg noodles for about 1-2 minutes.
2. Drain them well and keep everything aside.
3. In a large skillet, heat the oil on medium-high heat, sauté the onion and garlic for about 1 minute.
4. Stir in the bell pepper and broccoli and stir fry everything for about 3 minutes.
5. Stir in the remaining ingredients and cook for about 3 more minutes.
6. Serve the noodles with a topping of the veggie mixture.

Hearty
Chili Noodles Bake

Prep Time: 15 mins
Total Time: 50 mins

Servings per Recipe: 6
Calories   510 kcal
Fat   20 g
Carbohydrates   49 g
Protein   27.6 g
Cholesterol   111 mg
Sodium   1129 mg

Ingredients

1 (12 oz.) package wide egg noodles
1 lb. ground beef
1 onion, chopped
3 cloves garlic, minced
2 (15 oz.) cans tomato sauce
1 (8 oz.) can tomato sauce
15 fluid oz. water
1 C. broth

1 tbsp ground cumin
1 tsp dried oregano
1/2 tsp cayenne pepper
1 C. shredded sharp Cheddar cheese

Directions

1. Set your oven to 350 degrees F before doing anything else and grease a 14x9-inch baking dish.
2. In a large pan of lightly salted boiling water, cook the egg noodles for about 5 minutes, stirring occasionally.
3. Drain them well and keep everything aside.
4. Heat a large skillet on medium-high heat and cook the beef till browned completely.
5. Add the onion and garlic and stir fry them till the onion becomes tender.
6. Add the tomato sauce, broth, water, oregano, cumin and cayenne pepper and bring to a simmer.
7. Stir in the pasta and place the mixture into the prepared baking dish.
8. Top everything with the cheddar cheese and cook everything in the oven for about 20 minutes.

NOODLES
Russian Style

Prep Time: 10 mins
Total Time: 20 mins

Servings per Recipe: 6
Calories	363 kcal
Fat	24.2 g
Carbohydrates	27.1g
Protein	9.9 g
Cholesterol	78 mg
Sodium	394 mg

Ingredients

1 (8 oz.) package egg noodles
2 C. sour cream
1/2 C. grated Parmesan cheese, divided
1 tbsp chopped fresh chives
1/2 tsp salt

1/8 tsp ground black pepper
2 tbsp butter

Directions

1. In a large pan of lightly salted boiling water, cook the egg noodles for about 8-10 minutes.
2. Drain well.
3. Add the butter and stir to combine.
4. Meanwhile in a bowl, mix together 1/4 C. of the cheese, sour cream, chives, salt and black pepper.
5. Place the mixture over the noodles and gently, stir to combine.
6. Serve immediately with a topping of the remaining cheese.

Japanese Style
Egg Noodle

Prep Time: 10 mins
Total Time: 25 mins

Servings per Recipe: 6
Calories   152.2
Fat   5.4g
Cholesterol   15.9mg
Sodium   896.9mg
Carbohydrates   22.6g
Protein   4.3g

Ingredients

1/4 lb fine dried egg noodles
1 medium red onion, sliced thinly
1 1/2 C. fresh shiitake mushrooms, sliced thinly
1 tbsp vegetable oil
3 tbsp soy sauce
1 tbsp balsamic vinegar

2 tsp brown sugar
1 tsp salt
1 tbsp sesame oil
fresh parsley leaves, to garnish

Directions

1. In a large pan of lightly salted boiling water, cook the egg noodles for about 5 minutes.
2. Drain them well and keep everything aside.
3. In a large skillet, heat the oil and sauté the mushrooms and onion for about 3 minutes.
4. Stir in the noodles, brown sugar, vinegar, soy sauce and salt and toss to coat well.
5. Stir in the sesame oil and serve with a garnishing of parsley.

SOUTHWEST
Nachos

🍲 Prep Time: 10 mins
🕐 Total Time: 20 mins

Servings per Recipe: 1	
Calories	18.9
Fat	0.3g
Cholesterol	0.2mg
Sodium	14.8mg
Carbohydrates	3.4g
Protein	0.7g

Ingredients

1 C. diced tomatoes
1/4 C. diced green pepper
2 tbsp chopped ripe olives
2 tbsp chopped green chilies
2 tsp white vinegar
1/4 tsp garlic powder
1/8 tsp fresh ground pepper

corn tortilla chips
1/4 C. shredded low-fat sharp cheddar cheese
Corn Tortilla Chips
9 6-inch corn tortillas
cold water

Directions

1. Set your oven to 350 degrees F before doing anything else.
2. Dip the tortillas in the cold water and then drain them on paper towels.
3. Arrange the tortillas onto an ungreased baking sheet and cook everything in the oven for about 10 minutes.
4. Remove everything from the oven and keep it aside to cool.
5. With a biscuit cutter, cut the tortillas into 2 1/2-inch circles.
6. Now, set the oven to broiler and arrange the oven rack about 6-inches from the heating element.
7. In a large bowl, mix together the olives, green pepper, tomatoes, green chilies, garlic powder, black pepper and vinegar.
8. Place about 2 tsp of the vegetables mixture on each tortilla chips and cook everything under the broiler till the cheese is melted.

East LA Style
Nachos

Prep Time: 15 mins
Total Time: 1 hr

Servings per Recipe: 4

Calories	222.6
Fat	9.1g
Cholesterol	37.7mg
Sodium	85.0mg
Carbohydrates	23.1g
Protein	15.6g

Ingredients

2 boneless skinless chicken breasts, cut into small strips.
1/2 C. lime juice
1 tsp pepper
1 tsp chili powder
2 tbsp olive oil

1 C. frozen corn kernels
1/3 C. red onion, chopped
1 tbsp lime juice
1 tsp cumin
tortilla chips

Directions

1. In a bowl, mix together the chicken, olive oil, 1/4 C. of the lime juice, chili powder and black pepper and refrigerate to marinate for about 30 minutes.
2. Meanwhile, cook the corn till desired doneness.
3. In a bowl, add the onion, corn and the remaining lime juice and toss to coat.
4. Heat a large nonstick frying pan and cook the chicken till the desired doneness.
5. Transfer the chicken into the bowl, with the corn mixture and mix well.
6. Top the tortilla chips with the chicken mixture and serve.

MONTEREY CRAB
and Shrimp Nachos

Prep Time: 10 mins

Total Time: 26 mins

Servings per Recipe: 6
Calories   377.0
Fat   18.7g
Cholesterol   79.8mg
Sodium   1244.6mg
Carbohydrates   37.2g
Protein   17.4g

Ingredients

1/2 lb. imitation crabmeat, shredded
1/2 lb. shrimp, cooked and chopped
1/2 C. low-fat sour cream
1 (4 1/2 oz.) can green chilies, diced
1 tsp chili powder
1/2 tsp ground cumin
1/4 tsp salt

1 C. salsa
1 C. shredded Monterey jack pepper cheese
1/2 C. black olives
2 scallions, sliced
1 (8 1/2 oz.) bags tortilla chips

Directions

1. Set your oven to 350 degrees F before doing anything else.
2. Place half of the tortilla chips in the bottom of a 13x9-inch baking dish evenly.
3. Top the dish with the seafood mixture, followed by the salsa, cheese, olives and scallions.
4. Cook everything in the oven for about 16 minutes.

Printed in Great Britain
by Amazon

65366436R00034